In a Twinkle

Youthful Quilt Designs

In a twinkle
covers crinkle
snuggle deep
off to sleep

Kay Mackenzie

Kay Mackenzie

Special thanks

To so many people. No one gets anywhere alone. My husband, Dana Mackenzie, who has no issues with me spending my time quilting, writing, and illustrating instead of practicing domestic skills. Willie the papillon (the real quilt puppy) for keeping me company in the studio and pre-approving all of my quilts. Pattern testers Debra Hartman Foster, Cheryl Henriksen, Kirsten Jacobson-Croak, Guin Jenanyan, Ann Horner, Geri Patterson-Kutras, Carmel Reitman, and Claire Witherspoon.

Take it easy and make it fun

Good habits and techniques are outlined throughout the instructions, but perfection is neither a requirement nor a goal. These are not competition quilts; these are quilts to be quickly made, with enjoyment; to give you laughter, to please you; to make especially for the little loved ones in your life.

Contents

Yardage, tools & notions

Fabric requirements have been figured generously and rounded up to the next standard increment.

In addition to some easy specialty techniques, the projects all use rotary cutting and machine sewing. You'll need a rotary cutter with sharp blade, acrylic ruler, cutting mat, and basic sewing supplies, plus any additional materials and notions noted. When a "pointy implement for turning" is listed, this refers to any point turner that you may already have, or a makeshift implement from around the house. What you'll need is something with a fairly hard tip that is pointed but not sharp (and won't leave a mark).

A flannel design wall is very useful. You can also use the floor or the bed to lay out your project. These design spaces will enable your pets to pre-approve your layout and also ensure that lots of pet hair will be sewn into the quilt, giving it that authentic touch. Another helpful tool is a reducing glass, which can make some things pop out that you didn't notice before.

ISBN 0-9725852-1-4
©In a Twinkle: Youthful Quilt Designs
©2004 Kay Mackenzie. All rights reserved. Printed and bound in the U.S.A. Second Printing.

Quilt Puppy
Publications & Designs

P.O. Box 1241
Aptos, California 95001
www.quiltpuppy.com

For additional copies, please revisit your local quilt shop or go to www.quiltpuppy.com

General info & all that fun stuff

Wash, dry, and press your fabrics

There's no rule that says one must prewash. Some quilters consider the sizing a benefit.
I like the feel of clean fabric, and washing out the sizing can make it easier to find the grain.

Line up the grain

Sometimes fabric gets a little warped when it's
wound onto the bolt. It's important to line up the
grain before cutting. This is easily done with half-yard
pieces and can also be done with one-yard pieces. For
fat quarters, which have the selvage on one side only,
treat the opposite side like a selvage for this process,
as it is generally cut at an accurate parallel. Take a
look at it first to be sure.

The fabric should be freshly pressed, with no crease
down the middle. Fold it in half, aligning selvages
together evenly all along the top. Observe the fold.
Is it wavy and rippling? Even though selvages and raw
edges may be aligned, ripples along the fold mean the
grain isn't lined up.

Keeping the selvages together, slide them in opposite
directions until the fold at the bottom straightens out
and lies flat.

When cutting, use two lines of reference

Before making a rotary cutting stroke, always position
the ruler using at least two lines of reference. Ideally
these lines are perpendicular to one another—in
other words, at right angles. Two horizontal or two
vertical lines are also okay. They might be seam lines,
selvages, raw edges, or mat lines, depending on the
situation. Checking multiple lines of reference instead
of just one means more accurate placement of the
ruler, a more accurate cut, and squarer and truer
blocks.

Safety first

When using a rotary cutter, you must heed the sharpness of the blade. If using a cutter
with a manual blade extender, close the blade each and every time you put it down.

Always cut away from yourself, never toward yourself.
Don't scratch your nose with the cutter in your hand.
Make sure your fingertips are safely back from the edge of the ruler.
If you ever make a cut without the ruler, pull your other hand back first.
Train yourself to be aware of finger position and blade status at all times.
To be extra safe, wear hard shoes in case you drop the cutter.
Show the cutter to your spouse so that there are no attempts to slice cheese with it.
(This is no laughing matter.)

Straighten one end

If you have a large cutting mat and a long ruler, this can be done with the fabric folded in half. For a smaller ruler and mat, fold the fabric in half again, bringing the first fold up to align with the selvages.

Place the fabric on the mat and align the top and/or bottom with mat lines. Place the ruler near the right end of the fabric where the raggedness begins. Line up the ruler, checking two lines of reference. Apply light pressure to the ruler with a spread hand, then engage the blade and stroke from bottom to top with the cutter in the other hand, bearing against the ruler. Left-handed quilters, please use mirror-image reversal.

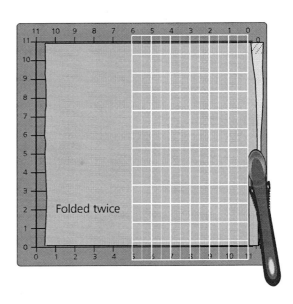

Folded twice

Measuring

Rotary cutting can be done using either the mat or the ruler as the measuring device. Check the ruler and mat against one another to make sure they measure the same. If there is any variance, choose one or the other and stick with it in the same project. If they match, you can use either strategy at will.

Measuring with the mat

To make it a little complicated, some manufacturers place the zero line at the right-hand side of the mat and some place it on the left. When the zero's on the left, it makes for an awkward initial trim, with the ruler hanging way off the mat and very little fabric under the ruler for it to grip. The zero on the top right is shown here. If you're a beginner and your mat has the left-hand zero, turn the mat upside down for now. After you've cut for awhile, you'll be able to use the mat however you like.

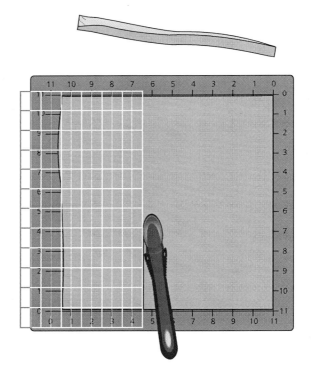

Right-zero cutting

The exposed fabric is what's being measured and cut. The mat lines are the measuring lines. The bulk of the material stays to the left. Line up the freshly trimmed straight end with the zero vertical line on the right-hand side of the mat, and align the top with a horizontal mat line. The ruler should extend above and below the fabric. After the first cut, leave the fabric in place and move the ruler to the left. If your mat isn't big enough, remove the first width and move the fabric over to the zero line again.

Unless you have an extra-big ruler, this method is more suitable for cutting wider widths.

In a Twinkle

Measuring with the ruler

Here, the fabric under the ruler is what's being measured and cut. The mat's main use is as a tabletop protector. After trimming the end, flip the fabric around so that the bulk is on the right. For extra precision, line up the top and left edge on the mat to create more lines of reference. Use the ruler for cutting placement. After the first cut, the ruler moves to the right, measuring from the cut edge each time. This method can be used to cut narrower widths like strips.

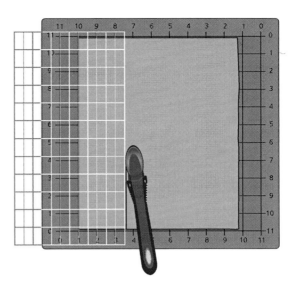

Cut widths, then patches

To cut squares and rectangles, stack cut widths and line them up horizontally on the mat with selvages extending past the zero line. The rotary cutter can cut through as many as eight layers, but four to six are easier. Trim off selvages, then cut widths into patches according to the project instructions.

The perfect quarter-inch seam

Let's take a moment to ponder that quilter's paragon, that vaunted ideal that we are sure everyone is achieving except us. I'm sorry to tell you this, but it doesn't exist. Cotton is a living, breathing thing, and cannot be rassled to complete and perfect obedience. Quilt Puppy motto: "Work toward perfection, remembering all the while that it cannot be achieved." We'll work toward quality results, enjoying the process without letting an unattainable goal disrupt our quilting pleasure.

Establish a good quarter-inch sewing method

Use the edge of a patchwork presser foot.
Cheat a little in from the edge of the patchwork presser foot.
Move the needle to the right until the edge of your regular foot is a ¼" guide.
Use the ¼" guide on the sewing-machine extension table, or make one with tape.

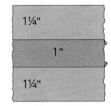

Seam test

Here's the test

Cut three strips of fabric about 6" long and 1½" wide. Sew them together the long way and press. If the center strip is exactly 1" wide, you have found a great method for sewing a ¼" seam. When piecing, take extra care not to wander at the beginning or end of seams. That's where it counts the most! Measuring your sewn units frequently will help produce a quilt top that's "crisp as a waffle and flat as a pancake."

A pressing issue

Using the iron to push your patches up and over is a recipe for distortion. Instead, place the sewn unit on the ironing board, flip the patch (or border), and finger-press all along the front of the seam. Crease lightly with your thumbnails in short strokes (don't stretch the fabric). Pat the unit down, making sure the seam is straight and fully extended. Then give it a light steam pressing to let it know you are serious.

Nestled seams

Sometimes it's called nestling, other times butting. During construction, when seams meet, the seam allowances need to fall in opposite directions so that they can snuggle up to one another and avoid adding bulk to the intersection. Plan your pressing so that seam allowances will nestle together cheerfully when joining units into sections or rows.

Stitch-pinning

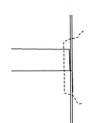

A great way to make sure your seams match up! When joining units into sections or rows, sew across only the nestled seams for the whole row, about ½" across each one, leaving the lengths in between unsewn. Check the stitch-pinning from the right side. If the intersections don't match up to your satisfaction, you can easily remove these few stitches and readjust. Then sew the entire seam, over the original stitches.

Appliqué and fun... the 2 words can be used together in a sentence

For these projects, you are welcome to use any form of appliqué that you may already be comfortable with. The instructions given employ fusible interfacing to create prepared-edge shapes, a method that works great for the simple motifs in these quilts. Nice shapes are easy to achieve, the edges are turned, and the motifs are held securely in place for topstitching or the appliqué stitch of your choice. Then the product is trimmed away, leaving no bulk or stiffness. You really will have fun with this, whether you're making lollipops, stars, hearts, or delectable dog bones!

For this method, you want to be sure you are using fusible interfacing, not "fusible web," which fuses on both sides. Fusible interfacing comes from the clothes-sewing world and has a smooth side and a slightly bumpy side. The bumpy side is the fusible side. The marking is done on the smooth, non-fusing side. When first using the product, take a moment to familiarize yourself with the feel of the two sides.

Adding simple borders

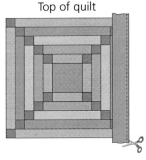

Top of quilt

For the simple framing borders in these small projects, we'll "sew, then trim." First, and important to the success of this approach, make sure the quilt is nicely squared up. Then extend a border strip beyond the top edge and sew it to the side of the quilt. Pinning is not necessary. Cut off any remaining length of border a little below the quilt. Add the other side border the same way. Flip the borders and press.

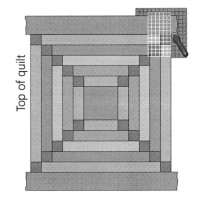

Top of quilt

Keeping the corners square, use the rotary cutter to trim the borders even with the quilt. Then add the top and bottom borders the same way. On the very last two borders of the quilt, backstitch at beginning and end.

Finishing your quilt

Here's where this little book leaves you with the famous phrase, "Quilt As Desired." Support your local quilt shop by checking there first for books and magazines with instructions on backing, layering, basting, quilting, binding, and labeling the youthful quilt you've made for someone dear at heart.

In a Twinkle

The Projects

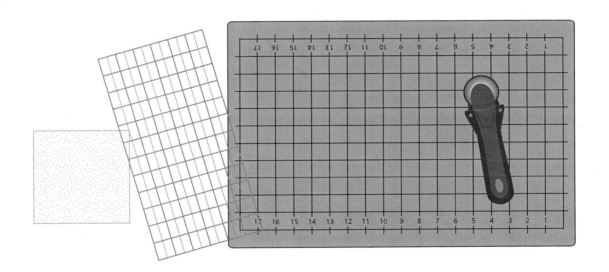

Comfy Cozy Blankie

Take advantage of today's fabulous flannels and make one of these soft, snuggly, reversible blankies in an afternoon. You'll quickly have a very cute gift that the new mom will love—and use! This un-quilt is great for throwing over a stroller, on the floor, or wrapping the little one up burrito-style.

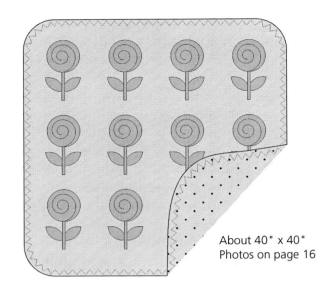

About 40" x 40"
Photos on page 16

Materials & notions

1¼ yards each of 2 coordinating cotton flannels
Thread for accent stitching (or 2 packs rickrack, optional)
Dinner plate
Pointy implement for turning

Instructions

Prewash the flannels in hot water and tumble dry. Smooth out the pieces and place them right sides together. Even up the ragged ends, straight across. Trim off the selvages. If one flannel is wider than the other, trim it to match the narrower one.

Place the dinner plate face down on each corner as shown and trace around the curve. Cut along the marked lines with scissors.

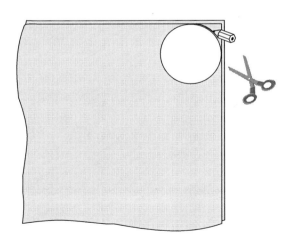

Backstitching at beginning and end, sew the flannels together with a ¼" seam, leaving an 8" gap on one side. Turn right-side-out through the gap. Insert the pointy implement and run it along the stitching line, fully extending the seam. Choose which flannel you like for the "A" side and press the edges so that the seam is slightly to the "B" side. Fold under the seam allowances of the unsewn portion and press.

Choose a decorative or zigzag stitch and sew around the perimeter of the blankie, about ¼" from the edge. Beside adding an attractive accent, this will flatten and reinforce the edges and close up the unsewn gap.

No fancy stitches? No zigzag? Use a double row of straight stitching—variegated thread looks nice—or sew purchased rickrack onto the "A" side with two rows of stitches.

That's it! So simple, yet guaranteed to be a big hit.

In a Twinkle

Lollipops, Candy Bars & Jujubes

A tasty confection of a quilt for wee little ones. Very easy to make—thanks to the use of lightweight fusible interfacing, you'll have fun with these lollipops. Classic pieced blocks in candy colors complete the sweet design.

39" x 43"
Photo on page 17
Detail on back cover

Materials & notions

5–10 candy fabrics	1¼ yards total
Background fabric	¾ yard
Inner border & sticks	⅓ yard
Outer border	¾ yard
Scrap fabric	(2) 7" squares

FYI: Backing will require 1½ yards

Sheer-to-lightweight fusible nonwoven interfacing (not fusible web) .... 1 yard

Threads to match or blend with candy fabrics
Pointy implement for turning

Cut these things

Candy fabrics	(10) 7" squares (assorted)
	(21) 2½" x 6½" rectangles (assorted)
	(8) sets of (5) 2½" squares (40 in all)
Background	(32) 2½" squares
	(10) 6½" x 8½" rectangles
Inner border/stick	(1) 1" strip x width of fabric
	(4) 2" strips x width of fabric
Outer border	(4) 3½" strips x width of fabric
Interfacing	(12) 7" squares

Make the jujube blocks

Using the 2½" squares, lay out one nine-patch and sew together as shown, alternating one set of candy squares with background squares. Press short seams toward the darker fabric. Press long seams away from the center.

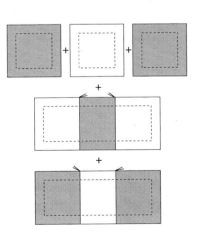

Inspector cluesew

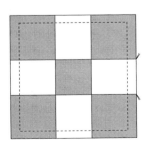

The block should measure 6½" square. If not, re-examine the size of your squares and seams. Make sure you're not wandering at the beginning or end of seams or doing "curvy" pressing. Now make the rest of the nine-patches.

Make the candy bar blocks

The good old Rail Fence block is the basis for the candy bars. Lay out the bars with the jujubes according to the diagram below, combining flavors as desired. Construct the blocks by sewing three bars together lengthwise. Press the seams toward the middle of the block.

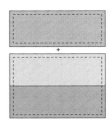

Construct the center

Join the blocks into rows. Press the block seams of the top and bottom rows in one direction, and the middle row in the opposite direction. Join the rows.

To aid with matching seams, use the stitch-pinning technique as described on page 6. Press the long row seams in whichever direction you like.

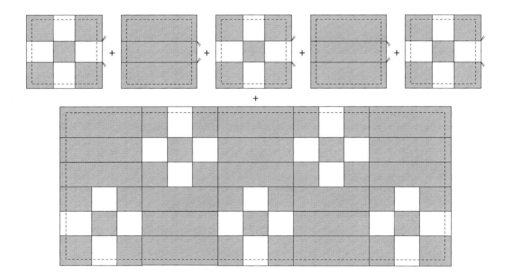

Now for the lollipops

They're easy and quick to make. Review the information on "appliqué and fun" on page 6.

First the sticks   Each stick will be ½" x 3¼"

From one 7" square of interfacing, cut five 1" strips. Take a moment to familiarize yourself with the feel of the interfacing, distinguishing between the smooth side and the slightly bumpy side. The bumpy side is the fusible side. Lay the strips end-to-end **smooth side up** on the **right side** of the 1" stick-fabric strip and sew each long side with a ¼" seam. Cut the strip apart where each piece of interfacing joins, then cut each 7" strip in half. With scissors, trim away about half of the seams on each side. You will now have ten 3½" trimmed fabric/interfacing strips.

If you have a loop turner or similar turning tool, use it now to push/pull one end through the middle of each tube and turn the sticks right-side-out. Or, attach a safety pin to the fabric on one end and push the pin through the tube. Be careful of the tender interfacing.

Once the sticks are turned, insert the pointy implement and slide it up and down the stitching lines to fully extend the seams. Finger-press well, but **do not press with an iron yet**. Trim each stick to 3¼".

In a Twinkle

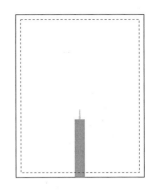

Turn on your iron. Fold a background rectangle in half lengthwise and finger-crease the lower portion. Lay it right-side-up on the ironing board, then center a stick right-side-up over the crease, lower edges aligned. Following the manufacturer's instructions for the interfacing, lower the iron onto the stick and press for the recommended length of time. Don't move the iron back and forth, just press by holding it in place. Steam is usually needed to activate the bonding agent, but again, check the instructions. Repeat for remaining lollipop blocks.

Stitch the sticks

If you are familiar with another form of machine appliqué, feel free to use it now to stitch the sticks to the background fabric. For super-simple topstitching, use thread that matches or blends with the stick fabric. Shorten your stitch length and sew on top of the stick, as close to the edge as possible.

Bright Idea

The sticks can be chain-stitched as follows: Turn the block upside down so that the stick is at the top. Beginning at the raw edges, stitch the right side of the stick, stopping with the needle down at the end. Lift the presser foot and pivot the block a quarter turn. Stitch across the top of the stick. Stop, pivot, and continue stitching down the other side of the stick. Do not cut the threads, but introduce the next block the same way you did the first and sew right onto it. When you pivot the second block, you can cut the two blocks apart. Sew all of the sticks this way.

Now,
Make a practice pop

Trace this circle onto the **smooth side** of a square of interfacing, using a fabric-friendly marking implement.

Note: If you can find something in your house that is a 5" circle, you can trace around it as an alternate marking method.

Place the marked interfacing square **smooth side up** on the **right side** of a scrap square. Pin the layers together in a few places. (After practicing, you may find you don't need the pins.)

You may photocopy this page for ease of use in your project.

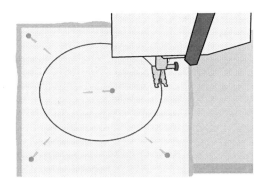
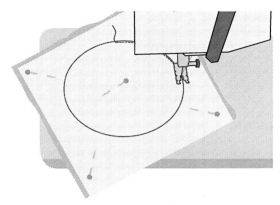

Sew around the circle just inside the marked line, sewing slowly with a short stitch length. Pivoting should not be necessary. Stop with the needle down when you need to pause and reposition your hands.

Try placing your left hand flat on the unit and rotating it counter-clockwise as you sew. If you have trouble, try sewing more slowly or adjusting the stitch length. Sew over the first few stitches when you come back to them.

Trim, slash, turn, and fuse

Trim the seam allowances to about ⅛". Pull the interfacing away from the fabric. Pinch a fold in the center of the interfacing and make a nip through it. Then lengthen the slash just enough to turn the pop right-side-out through the opening. Once the pop is turned, insert the pointy implement through the opening and run it along the stitching line, fully extending the seam and smoothing the curve. The pop will be a little puffy, but do not press with an iron until you're ready to fuse.

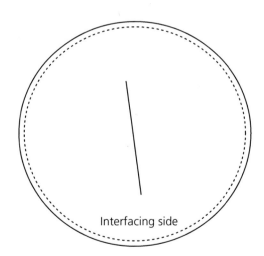

Interfacing side

Trim seam and slash interfacing

Fabric side

Turn pop and extend seam with pointy implement

Now turn on your iron. Place the practice pop, fabric side up, on the right side of the other scrap square. Fuse the pop down, following the manufacturer's instructions for the interfacing. Don't move the iron back and forth, just press by holding it in place. Reposition the iron until all of the pop is flattened and fused. Let cool briefly, then inspect the results. The fabric should cover the interfacing. If the interfacing is showing more than is attractive, it may mean you'll need to pull the edges of the slash together with a couple of large basting stitches, to make sure the interfacing stays under the fabric.

In a Twinkle

Proceed with the pops

Now make the ten candy pops, basting the slashes if necessary. Place a pop on the right side of a background rectangle. The pop should be centered over the stick, covering the end, and an equal distance from the top and the sides of the block. If using a directional fabric, make sure it is oriented the way you like. Fuse the ten candy pops.

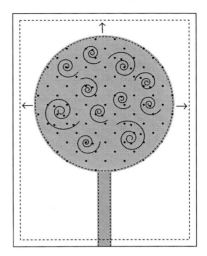

Stitch 'em

Starting at the bottom of the pop, topstitch as before (or use the machine appliqué method of your choice). Sew slowly and use a short stitch length. Pivoting should not be necessary. Halfway around, stop with the needle down and clip the beginning threads. When you return to the initial stitches, sew over a few stitches, then backstitch to secure the threads.

Remove fused background

Since the interfacing is fused to the background fabric, not to the pop, we can now remove the extra layer behind the pops. Pull the fused background away from the pop. Pinch a fold in the background and make a nip through it. Use scissors to carefully trim away the fused background fabric/interfacing. Leave about a scant ¼" margin, or enough to cover the turned edge of the pop.

Join lollipops to quilt

Referring to the illustration or photo, lay out lollipops as desired with the quilt interior, five on top going up and five at the bottom going down. Sew the pops into rows, pressing seams so that they will nestle when sewn to the quilt. Join the lollipop rows to the quilt, using the stitch-pinning technique.

Add borders

Add the inner and outer borders as described on page 6. Press the seams toward the inner border.

Rounding off

This quilt looks really nice with rounded corners. (Note: This will require bias binding for finishing, so if you are bias-averse, it will probably be better to keep your corners square.) Before quilting, place a dinner plate on each corner as shown and trace around the curve. Keep your quilting inside the lines. Before binding, cut along the marked lines.

Sweet!

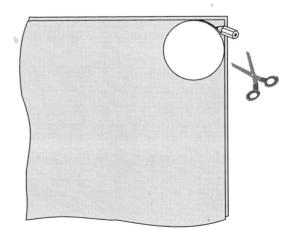

Giant Steps

Add chain squares to a giant Courthouse Steps block, make it in colors and fabrics that say "kid" and you've got Giant Steps! Fabric requirements given are for a quilt where each row is different. You may choose to repeat fabrics instead, or, for a less controlled look, mix fabrics in the rows.

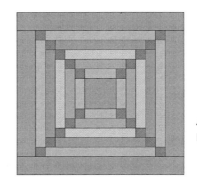

42½" x 42½"
Photos on pages 15 & 18

Fabric requirements

Center	8½" square
Chain squares.....	¼ yard (skinny or fat)
Row 1	¼ yard (skinny or fat)
Row 2.................	¼ yard (skinny or fat)
Row 3.................	¼ yard (skinny or fat)
Row 4.................	½ yard
Row 5.................	½ yard
Borders..............	¾ yard

FYI: Backing will require 1½ yards

Instructions

The information on pressing, nestled seams, stitch-pinning, and borders on pages 5–6 will be useful for this project.

Row 1: Sew side strips to center square. Flip strips over and press. Sew chain squares to either end of top and bottom strips. Press seams toward center of strip.

Lay top and bottom strips face down on center unit in position for sewing. Match the seams, then confirm the fit of the lengths in between. If one is more than ¹/₁₆" longer than the other, take a moment to measure and figure out whether it's the strip or the center unit that's off. Correcting the problem won't take long.

Once the strips and the center unit match up, stitch-pin the seams, then sew the strips to the center unit. Flip and press.

Now square up the corners. Align the 2¾" marks on your ruler with the horizontal and vertical corner seams. Trim the chain squares if necessary.

Add rows 2–5 the same way. To keep the presser foot from pushing the top layer along, start using real pins in between the stitch-pinning on about Row 3.

Cut these things

Center square..........	(1) 8½" square
Chain squares.........	(20) 3" squares
Row 1	(4) 3" x 8½" strips
Row 2.....................	(4) 3" x 13½" strips
Row 3.....................	(4) 3" x 18½" strips
Row 4.....................	(4) 3" x 23½" strips
Row 5.....................	(4) 3" x 28½" strips
Borders....................	(4) 5" strips x width of fabric

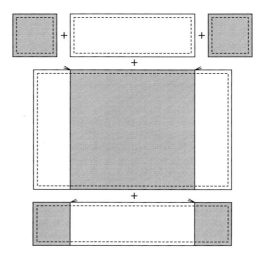

After Row 5, add borders as described on page 6. Before adding the top and bottom borders, check to make sure they will yield 42½" of usable length, or enough to go across the quilt side to side. If not, trim the side borders a little bit. Trim the same amount from the width of the top and bottom borders. Once any adjustments are completed, add the top and bottom borders. Flip, press, and trim.

Now ready for finishing, this cute quilt with a classic, time-honored look is sure to be warmly welcomed into any family.

In a Twinkle

Giant Steps

42 ½" x 42 ½"

Instructions on page 14.

This simple charmer was inspired by a picture of a feedsack quilt made in 1940. The classic, old-timey design combines wonderfully with the comforting palette of reproduction fabrics.

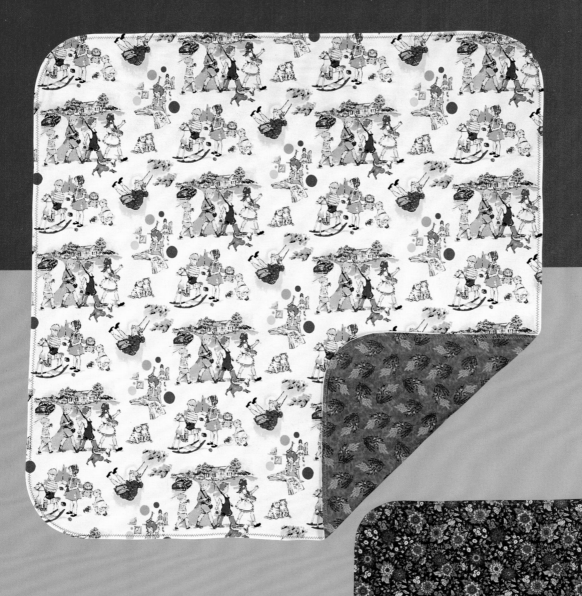

Comfy Cozy Blankie

about 40" x 40"

Choose a coordinating pair of today's fabulous flannels and make a warm, snuggly un-quilt in an afternoon.

Instructions on page 8.

In a Twinkle

Lollipops, Candy Bars & Jujubes

39" x 43"

Instructions on page 9.

Assorted candy colors make a truly scrumptious treat for a sweet little someone.

Star of My Heart
41" x 41"

No templates, no bias edges, and no appliqué expertise needed!

Instructions on page 19.

Giant Steps
42½" x 42½"

This cheerful version demonstrates how a vibrant, graphic look can be achieved using alternating colorways.

Instructions on page 14.

In a Twinkle

Star of My Heart

Thanks to some way cool techniques, this project goes together with ease. Nothing here is difficult, so have loads of fun creating a quilt that declares what everyone knows... little folks are always the stars of the heart. (The quilt puppy says, little dogs too.)

41" x 41"
Photos on page 18
and inside back cover

Design options

In one option, the background is all the same fabric, with narrow strips outlining the squares in the design, as seen in the illustration above and in the blue and pink quilt on page 18. A different way to make the squares show up is to use a somewhat contrasting fabric behind the heart-stars, as in the Americana version inside the back cover. For this option, you'll need ¾ yard of background fabric and ¾ yard of a different value or color for the 9½" squares. The strips can be eliminated.

Materials & notions

Background	1½ yards total (see design options)
Banners/strips	¾ yard
Stars	¾ yard
Hearts/border	¾ yard
Scrap fabric	(1) 5" square & (2) 8½" squares

FYI: Backing will require 1¼ yards

Sheer-to-lightweight nonwoven fusible interfacing (not fusible web)........ 1 yard

Threads to match star, heart, and strip fabrics
Fabric-friendly marker for tracing
Pointy implement for turning

Cut these things

Background	(5) 9½" squares (see design options)
	(8) 3½" x 9½" rectangles
	(8) 3½" x 12½" rectangles
	(4) 3½" squares
Banners	(4) 3½" x 12½" rectangles
	(16) 3½" squares
Strips	(16) 1" x 9½" strips (see design options)
Stars	(5) 8½ " squares
Hearts	(5) 5" squares
Border	(4) 4½" strips x width of fabric
Interfacing	(6) 8½" squares and (6) 5" squares

Instructions

We'll begin with the heart-star blocks. Please review the information on "appliqué and fun" on page 6.

Make a practice star

Trace the star onto the **smooth side** of one of the large interfacing squares. Place the marked square **smooth side up** on the **right side** of a large scrap square. Sew just inside the marked line, going slowly with a shortened stitch length. At the inner notches, stop with the needle down, lift the presser foot, and pivot. At the star points, stop with the needle down, pivot halfway, sew one stitch across, then pivot again and keep sewing. (This gives the point a little room for the seam allowance once the shape is turned. I learned this in 8th-grade home-ec class.) Continue on around the star, sewing over the first few stitches when you come back to them.

Trim the seam allowances to about $1/8$". In the notches, clip almost to the stitching line. At the points, trim straight across and then taper the seam allowances toward the tip just a little more. Pull the interfacing away from the fabric. Pinch a fold in the center of the interfacing and make a nip through it. Then lengthen the slash just enough to turn the star right-side-out through the opening. Once the star is turned, push the points out as far as you can with your fingers, then insert the pointy implement and gently poke the star points out. Be careful of the tender interfacing, and don't be a pointiness overachiever. The tips will never be quite as pointy as the printed pattern.

You may photocopy this page for ease of use in your project.

The star will be a little puffy after turning, but do not press with an iron just yet.

In a Twinkle

Now turn on your iron. Place the star, fabric side up, on the right side of the other large scrap square. Following the manufacturer's instructions for the interfacing, lower the iron onto the star and press for the recommended length of time. Don't move the iron back and forth, just press by holding it in place. Reposition the iron until all of the star is flattened and fused. Let cool, then inspect the results. The fabric should cover the interfacing. If the interfacing is showing more than is attractive, it may mean you'll need to pull the edges of the slash together with a couple of large basting stitches, to make sure the interfacing stays under the fabric.

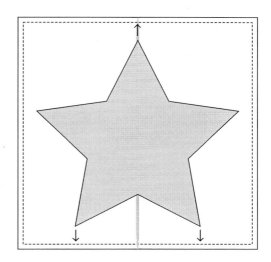

Proceed with the stars

Now make the five stars for the project, basting the slashes if necessary. Fold the 9½" background squares in half lengthwise and crease. Center the stars on the squares and fuse.

Stitch 'em

If you are familiar with another form of machine appliqué, feel free to use it now to stitch the stars. For super-simple topstitching, use thread that matches or blends with the star. With the same shortened stitch length, sew on top of the star, as close to the edge as possible. Pivot at the notches as before. Be sure to stitch the rounded tips down well with a stitch-pivot-stitch technique. About halfway around the star, stop and clip the beginning threads. When you return to the initial stitches, sew over a few stitches, then backstitch to secure the threads.

Trim 'em

Since the interfacing is fused to the background fabric, not to the stars, we can now remove the extra layer behind the stars.

Pull the fused background layer away from the star. Pinch a fold in the background and make a nip through it. Taking care not to cut the star, use scissors to trim away the fused background layer. Leave about a scant ¼ " margin, or enough to cover the turned edge of the star. Repeat for the remaining stars.

Make a practice heart

Trace the heart onto the **smooth side** of a small interfacing square. Place the marked square **smooth side up** on the **right side** of the small scrap square.

Sew the heart as you did the star, going slowly with a shortened stitch length. Stitch around the curves as much as possible. On the curviest parts, stop with the needle down and pivot slightly every 2–3 stitches. If you have trouble, try going more slowly or adjusting the stitch length.

Trim the seam allowances to about ⅛". In the notch, clip almost to the stitching line. At the point, trim straight across and then taper the seam allowances toward the tip just a little more.

Slash and turn as you did for the stars. Use the pointy implement to gently poke the point out and extend the seam, smoothing the curves. Center the heart on the practice star, fuse, and check to make sure the interfacing isn't peeking out.

Trimmed and clipped,
ready to slash and turn

Proceed with the hearts

Now make the five hearts for the project, basting the slashes if necessary. Center the hearts on the stars. Fuse, stitch, and trim away the background layer as before.

Add the outlining strips Skip this step if using a different background fabric for the heart-star blocks.

The center block does not need strips, so set one of the heart-star blocks aside. For the remaining blocks, fold the 1" strips in half lengthwise, wrong sides together, and press. Lay a folded strip on the right side of a block, raw edges aligned. Using thread that matches or blends with the strip, topstitch the fold as close to the edge as possible, or stitch the fold down with the method you have been using. (It's important to stitch the fold, as opposed to creating a free flange, so that little fingers and toes won't get caught.) Repeat for the other side. To reduce bulk, trim the middle layer close to the stitching line. Add the top and bottom strips the same way. The completed block, still 9½" unfinished size, is shown at the bottom of page 19.

Make the banner units

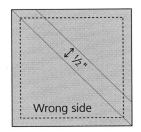

Wrong side

To avoid working with bias edges, we'll use the nifty "snowball" maneuver. (If this technique causes you concern over fabric waste, you'll receive a really cool surprise.) Begin by marking a diagonal line from corner to corner on the wrong side of the 3½" banner squares. Mark another diagonal line ½" away.

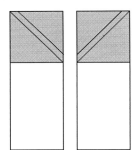

Lay out the eight 9½" rectangles, right sides up. Place a square face down at the top of each rectangle, edges aligned. Orient half of the diagonals one way, and half the other way. The extra line is always on top. Sew each unit on both marked lines.

Flip the lower portions of the squares up and finger-press to verify that they are in place correctly, covering the entire corner of the rectangles.

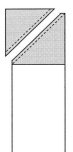

Lay the squares back down and cut between the stitching lines. Set aside the parts you have cut off. Flip the corners back up and press.

Repeat for the 12½" rectangles.

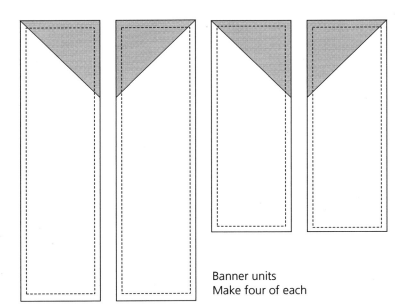

Banner units
Make four of each

Lay out

The interior of the quilt is constructed in three sections, as shown in the diagram below. The block without strips goes in the center. In preparation for joining units, now is a good time to review the information on pressing and stitch-pinning on pages 5–6.

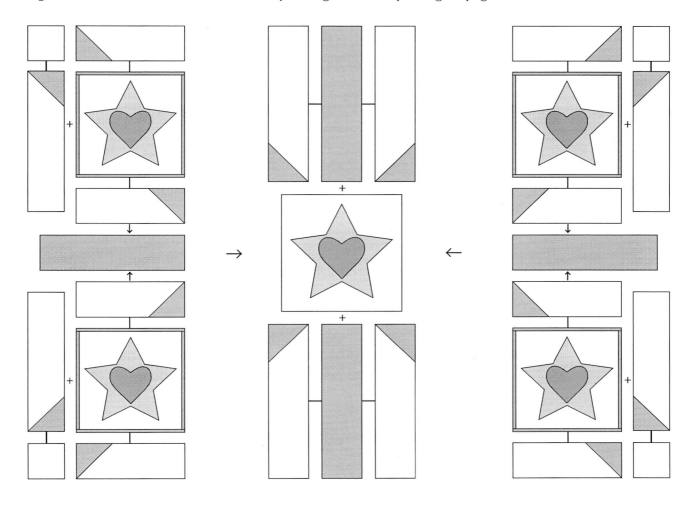

Construction & pressing

First join the units that are shown connected with lines. Then join combined units as indicated by plus signs. Then join as indicated by arrows.

Right and left sections... press toward banner units.
Center section... press away from banner units.
Joining sections... press toward center of quilt.

Borders

Add borders as described on page 6. Now this heartfelt little quilt that only looks complicated is ready for your finishing touches.

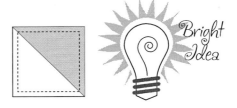

By sewing that extra diagonal line, we turned the cut-off parts into ready-made half-square triangles for use in another project! Press open and square up before using.

Puppy Doodles

Let the fabric speak! A framed fat quarter featuring your favorite cavorting canine is accented with woofy mottos and a sprinkle of decorations with dog appeal.

The quilt puppy, who has cats of his own, says you can use this to make a Kitten Kaboodles quilt too. Just substitute feline fabric, meow-language, and draw some simple shapes that are quintessentially catty, like fish or mice, to make the decorations.

Don't stop there... use the road map to design any theme quilt you like. The shapes you draw don't need to be sophisticated or detailed.

36" x 46"
Photos inside
back cover

Materials & notions

Dog fabric (center panel) .... Fat quarter*
   *Or a 15½" wide x 17½" high piece
Frame .... ½ yard
Motto panels .... ½ yard
Bones .... (2) 6" x 11" rectangles
Balls, assorted .... (6) 5" squares
Inner border .... ½ yard
Outer border .... ¾ yard
Scrap fabric .... (2) 5" squares

FYI: Backing will require 1½ yards

Sheer-to-lightweight fusible nonwoven interfacing (not fusible web) .... ¾ yard

Permanent fabric marker for inking mottos
Threads to match or blend with bones and balls
Pointy implement for turning

Cut these things

Dog fabric .... (1) piece 15½" wide x 17½" high*
   *If using a directional print, note the orientation

Frame .... (1) 5" strip x width of fabric
   .... (2) 4" strips x width of fabric

Motto panels ...... (2) 5½" strips x width of fabric

Bones .... (2) 6" x 11" rectangles

Balls .... (6) 5" squares

Inner border .... (4) 2½" strips x width of fabric

Outer border ...... (4) 4½" strips x width of fabric

Interfacing .... (2) 6" x 11" rectangles
   .... (7) 5" squares

General instructions

The frame, motto panels, and borders are all added using the easy "sew, then trim" approach. Now is a good time to review "Adding simple borders" on page 6.

Frame the center panel

Using the 5" frame strip, add one side of the frame to the center panel. Use the rest of the strip for the other side. Then use the 4" frame strips for the top and bottom.

Equal time, please

In a Twinkle

Motto panels

Fold the panels in half lengthwise and finger-crease. Center, trace, and ink your favorite dog sayings onto the panels using a permanent fabric marker.

Feel free to make up your own expression, or use your dog's name. (He or she will like that.) Matching centers, add top and bottom panels and trim excess.

Decorations

These primitive shapes are easy to accomplish using fusible interfacing. Please review the information on "appliqué and fun" on page 6.

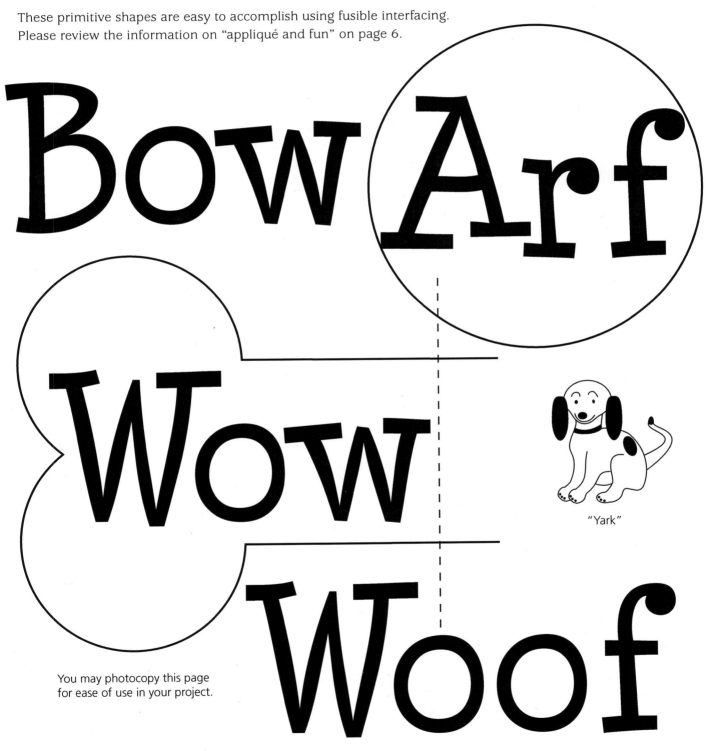

"Yark"

You may photocopy this page for ease of use in your project.

Make the balls and bones

Start by making a practice ball. Using a fabric-friendly marker, trace the circle on the previous page onto the **smooth side** of an interfacing square. Place the marked interfacing **smooth side up** on the **right side** of a scrap square. Pin the layers together. (After practicing, you may find you don't need pins.)

The instructions are the same as for the pops in *Lollipops, Candy Bars, & Jujubes*. Please turn to page 12 and follow the instructions there for stitching, trimming, turning, and fusing your practice ball.

Once you are familiar with the method, go ahead and make all of the balls for the project, basting the slashes if necessary. Remember, do not press them with an iron until later, when they are placed on the project and ready to fuse.

Trace the dog bone half, plus the dashed line, onto one end of the **smooth side** of an interfacing rectangle. Rotate the interfacing (do not turn it over), line it up, and trace the other half.

Place the marked interfacing **smooth side up** on the **right side** of a bone rectangle. Sew just inside the line, going slowly with a short stitch length. Sew around the curves as much as possible. If necessary, stop with the needle down, lift the presser foot, and pivot slightly every 2–3 stitches. Pivot at the notches. Sew over the first few stitches when you return to them.

Clip the notches almost to the stitching line. Trim, slash, and turn the bone. Baste the edges of the interfacing together to prevent gaping in the narrow shank area. Repeat for the other bone.

Proceed with the decorations

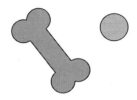

Place the decorations as desired, fabric side up, on the frames and motto panels. A sprinkled or tossed effect is nice, with some of the motifs crossing the seams. Fuse the decorations in place.

Stitch 'em

If you are familiar with another form of machine appliqué, feel free to use it now. For super-simple topstitching, use thread that matches or blends with the motif. With the same shortened stitch length, sew on top of the motif, as close to the edge as possible.

Fold or roll the unit as needed to pass through the throat of the machine. Halfway around each shape, stop and clip the beginning threads. When you return to the initial stitches, sew over a few stitches, then backstitch to secure the threads.

Remove fused background

Since the interfacing is fused to the background, not to the bones and balls, we can now remove the extra layer behind them. Pull the fused background away from the motif. Pinch a fold in the background and make a nip through it. Taking care not to cut the motif, use scissors to trim away the fused background layer. Leave about a scant ¼" margin, or enough to cover the turned edge of the motif.

Add borders

Now add the inner and outer borders. Press the seams toward the inner border.

Biscuit for you!

That's all it takes for an easy little theme quilt that will make people smile.

In a Twinkle

An assortment of night-sky fabrics that are close in value will create a serene, blended field for the brighter heavenly-body design elements.

Materials & notions

Night-sky fabrics, assorted.......	1¾ yards total
Stars, assorted	(5) 8½" squares
Moon...	(1) 8" x 10" rectangle
Quilt patches, assorted	⅓ yard total
Pillow	(1) 4" x 8" rectangle
Bed	¼ yard (skinny)
Inner border...........................	½ yard
Scrap fabric	(2) 8½" squares

FYI: Backing will require 1¾ yards plus (probably) material added to make it a little wider

Sheer-to-lightweight fusible nonwoven interfacing (not fusible web)......................1¼ yard

Permanent fabric marker for inking letters
Threads to match or blend with stars, moon, & pillow
Freezer paper, 4"x 8" piece
Sandpaper
Pointy implement for turning

The sky

For the main sky section, lay out twenty of the night-sky squares as desired in four rows of five.

Below the main section, lay out the parts of the sky that fall within the pillow row, as shown. Use the same fabric for the two patches on the far left.

When satisfied with the placement, join the squares in the main section into rows. (Don't sew the pillow row yet.) To allow nestling, press the seams in rows 1 and 3 in the same direction, and 2 and 4 in the opposite direction. Sew the four rows together. The stitch-pinning technique described on page 6 is very useful for making sure the seams match up.

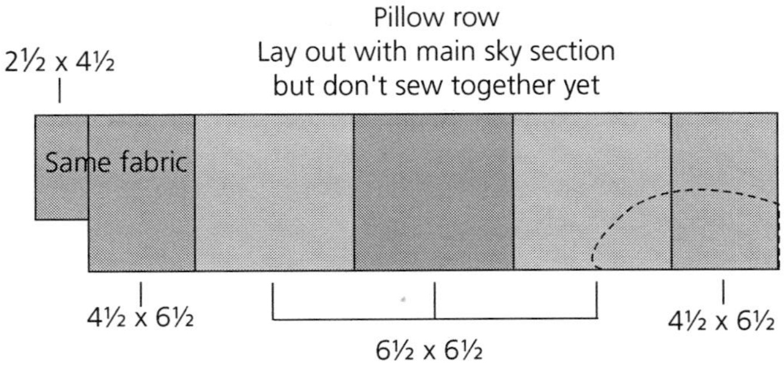

In a twinkle covers crinkle snuggle deep off to sleep

43" x 53"
Cover quilt

Full view inside front cover

Cut these things

Night-sky fabrics............	(23) 6½" squares
....	(2) 4½" x 6½" rectangles
....	(3) 2½" x 6½" rectangles
....	(3) 2½" x 4½" rectangles
Save the rest of the fabrics...borders will be cut later	
Stars	(5) 8½" squares
Moon...............................	(1) 8" x 10" rectangle
Quilt patches	(39) 2½" squares
Pillow	(1) 4" x 8" rectangle
Bed	(1) 2½" x 26½" strip
....	(1) 2½" x 16½" strip
....	(1) 2½" x 12½" strip
Inner border.................	(4) 3" strips x width of fabric
Interfacing.......................	(6) 8½" squares
....	(1) 8" x 10" rectangle

Pillow row
Lay out with main sky section but don't sew together yet

2½ x 4½

Same fabric

4½ x 6½

6½ x 6½

4½ x 6½

The pillow

Join the two sky patches that lie underneath the pillow. Press the seam in the direction that will allow it to nestle with the last row of the main sky section.

Then prepare the pillow. The right and lower edges will be sewn into seams, so only the curved upper edge needs to be turned. Here's an easy way to get the pillow ready, using a freezer-paper template and a little hand-basting.

Trace the pillow onto the **paper side** of the freezer paper and cut out on the marked line. Place the pillow fabric **right side up** on the ironing board. Lay the template **paper side up** on top. Press with a dry iron just until the freezer paper adheres.

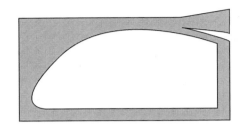

Allow to cool briefly, then trim the fabric around the template, **leaving a ¼" margin** all the way around.

Remove the template. Holding the pillow with the right side toward you, fold the seam allowance to the back (eyeballing works fine) and hand-baste about $1/8$" from the turned edge. Only do the top of the pillow, continuing all the way around the front curve. Leave the right and lower edges unturned. Press the pillow, creasing the turned edge well.

Pin the pillow onto the joined sky patches, aligning right and lower raw edges. If you are familiar with another form of machine appliqué, feel free to use it now to stitch the turned edge of the pillow. For super-simple topstitching, use thread that matches or blends with the pillow. With a shortened stitch length, sew on top of the turned edge of the pillow, as close to the edge as possible. Remove the basting thread. Turn the unit over and trim away the sky layer underneath the pillow, leaving a scant ¼" margin.

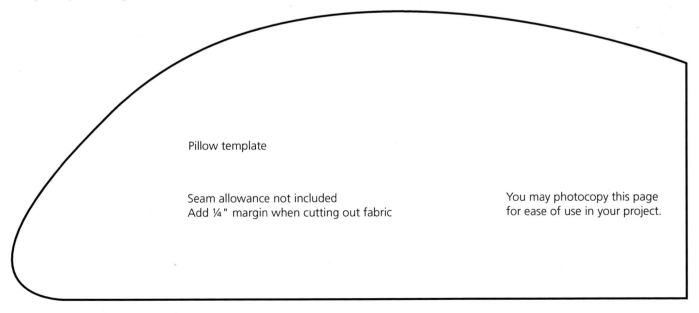

Pillow template

Seam allowance not included
Add ¼" margin when cutting out fabric

You may photocopy this page for ease of use in your project.

The bed

Next comes the bed section. We'll start with the part between the bedposts. Beneath the pillow row, lay out the quilt patches as desired in three rows of thirteen, then the 26½" bed strip, then the lower sky patches.

Sew each row together. Press pillow row to nestle with main sky section. Press remaining rows to allow nestling. Then join rows as shown at right. Press long seams toward the bed strip.

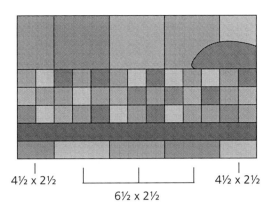

4½ x 2½   6½ x 2½   4½ x 2½

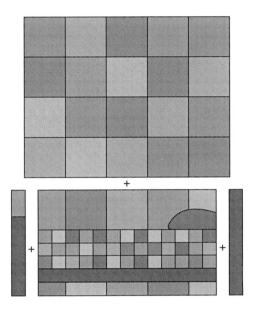

Sew the last sky patch to the foot of the bed, then add the head and foot of the bed to the center bed section. Press seams toward bed strips.

Join the main sky section to the bed section.

The poem

The inner border presents a lovely opportunity to embellish the quilt with a poem, a name, a bedtime expression, or the sentiment of your choice. If you like my little rhyme, it's given on the following page in actual size. The instructions that follow will be referring to it. Feel free to follow the general instructions using your own expression printed out in very large type, or do the inking freehand if that is among your skills. Any alternative way your creativity leads you to embellish the border, go for it!

This inking is quite easy to accomplish, and takes just a few minutes. Don't agonize over achieving perfect tracing results. Even if your letters don't match the type exactly, the end result will still look great.

For the inking process, I recommend tracing all of the hearts and letters first. Then place the border on sandpaper and finish filling in the figures.

Fold one of the inner border strips in half crosswise and lengthwise and crease. Line up the vertical crease with the center of the heart and trace the heart.

Line up the horizontal crease with the dashed lines for each section of the poem. Putting a heart between each section, trace backward from the central heart for the first part of the poem (*covers crinkle*, then *In a twinkle*). Trace forward for the last part (*snuggle deep*, then *off to sleep*).

In a twinkle

♥

covers crinkle

snuggle deep

off to sleep

Inner border

After finishing the inner border embellishment, refer to the information on page 6 about adding borders using the "sew, then trim" approach. Add any unembellished borders in this fashion, sides first and then top and bottom. For embellished borders, match the center of the border to the center of the quilt before sewing. Press seams toward borders.

The stars

Please review the information on "appliqué and fun" on page 6. The template and the instructions are the same as for *Star of My Heart*. Turn to page 20 and make a practice star as described there, through the first paragraph on page 21.

Once you've completed your practice star and have become familiar with the method, go ahead and make the five stars for the project. Remember, do not press them with an iron yet.

The moon

Trace, stitch, trim, and turn the moon the same way. Pull the edges of the slash together with a couple of large basting stitches, to make sure the interfacing stays under the fabric.

Heavenly bodies

Place the stars and moon as desired in the night sky. It's always a nice surprise when design elements leap out of their containers, so consider crossing onto the inner border and down into the pillow row as well. Fuse the motifs in place, then refer to the instructions on page 21 for stitching the heavenly bodies, folding or rolling the unit as needed to pass through the throat of the machine.

After stitching, pull the fused background layer away from the motifs. Pinch a fold in the background and make a nip through it. Taking care not to cut the motifs, use scissors to trim away the fused background layer. Leave about a scant ¼" margin, or enough to cover the turned edge of the motifs.

Outer borders

Bring out your leftover night-sky fabrics and cut rectangles that are 4½" wide and of various lengths, whatever the pieces will yield. Lay them out all around the quilt as desired for this improvisational composed border.

Construct the sides first. Sew together enough rectangles to make side borders that are the same length or a little longer than the sides of the quilt. Add them using the "sew, then trim" method, pressing seams toward the inner border.

Construct the top and bottom borders. Add them to the quilt the same way.

Now to bed, and sleep well.

Moon template

Note: Template is reversed, as the interfacing method produces a mirror image of asymmetrical shapes

You may photocopy this page for ease of use in your project.

The Particulars

The quilts

All designs by Kay Mackenzie.

All quilts made and machine-quilted by Kay using White Rose 100% Cotton Needled Batting from Mountain Mist; www.mountainmistlp.com.

Lollipops, Candy Bars & Jujubes features fabrics from the Color Tree collection by Jason Yenter for In The Beginning Fabrics; www.inthebeginningfabrics.com.

Giant Steps on page 15 features fabrics from various Aunt Grace collections by Judie Rothermel for Marcus Brothers Textiles, Inc.; www.marcusbrothers.com.

The tools

Kay uses pressure-sensitive Omnigrid® and Dritz® rotary cutters; www.dritz.com.

The product used for the appliqué was Pellon® 906F, Fusible Nonwoven Interfacing for Sheer to Lightweight Fabrics; www.pellonideas.com.

Marvy® Fabric Markers were used for inking.

The author

Kay Mackenzie caught the quilt pox twelve years ago and has been working on a quilting project or eight ever since. A specialist in hand appliqué and miniatures, Kay has brought home numerous awards from judged competitions. You are invited to view a gallery of her work at www.quiltpuppy.com.

Now Kay combines her love for quilting with her writing and illustrating skills in Quilt Puppy Publications & Designs.

Kay lives with her husband, science journalist Dana Mackenzie, Willie (the real quilt puppy), and three cats in Santa Cruz, California.

The book

Design, illustrations, and layout by Kay Mackenzie using Adobe® Illustrator®, Photoshop®, and InDesign® on a souped-up blueberry iMac.

Photography by Tony Grant, Santa Cruz.

Printed by Community Printers, Santa Cruz; www.comprinters.com.

Title and heading typeface is Frivolous (Typadelic). Text is Usherwood (ITC-Adobe). Captions are Frutiger (Linotype AC-Adobe). Dog mottos are Minya Nouvelle (Larabie). Poem is Harrington (Font Bureau-Microsoft).

Where credit is gratefully due

Kay's friend Carmel Reitman taught her and the other Nite Needlers how to make the Comfy Cozy Blankie.

Kay learned about fusible interfacing appliqué during a demo by cartoonist, quilter, fabric designer, and neighbor Ellen Edith. Check out her whimsical creations at www.ellenedith.com.

Years ago the stitch-pinning technique (though it wasn't called that) was discovered in the book *Tips for Quilters* by Rachel T. Pellman. Thank you, Susan M. Miller of Centreville, Maryland.

Kay's other book

Dog Cabin and Others: A Fast Fun Theme-Quilt Project from Quilt Puppy Publications & Designs is great for beginners and experienced quilters alike.

Use your favorite theme from today's novelty fabrics to make a refreshingly fast, fun, and easy quilt top. No templates, no pinning, no fuss. Just cut, sew, and trim as you go. Accuracy without agony!

Ask for it at your favorite quilt shop or visit www.quiltpuppy.com.

In a Twinkle